Instant Messaging

FOR

DUMMIES®

Pocket Edition

**by John R. Levine,
Margaret Levine Young, and
Carol Baroudi**

**Edward C. Baig and
Bob LeVitus**

**Robert Kao and
Dante Sarigumba**

D1242264

Instant Messaging For Dummies® Pocket Edition

Published by
Wiley Publishing, Inc.
111 River Street
Hoboken, NJ 07030-5774
www.wiley.com

Copyright © 2008 by Wiley Publishing, Inc., Indianapolis, Indiana

Published by Wiley Publishing, Inc., Indianapolis, Indiana

Published simultaneously in Canada

For general information on our other products and services, please contact our Customer Care Department within the U.S. at 800-762-2974, outside the U.S. at 317-572-3993, or fax 317-572-4002.

For technical support, please visit www.wiley.com/techsupport.

Wiley also publishes its books in a variety of electronic formats. Some content that appears in print may not be available in electronic books.

ISBN: 978-0-470-22414-4

Manufactured in the United States of America

Contents at a Glance

Publisher's Acknowledgments

We're proud of this book; please send us your comments through our online registration form located at www.dummies.com/register/.

Some of the people who helped bring this book to market include the following:

Acquisitions, Editorial, and Media Development

Project Editors: Mark Enochs, Susan Pink

Acquisitions Editors: Greg Croy, Steven Hayes, Bob Woerner

Copy Editors: Heidi Unger, Rebecca Whitney

Editorial Managers: Leah Cameron, Jodi Jensen

Composition Services

Project Coordinator: Kristie Rees

Layout and Graphics: Carl Byers

Proofreader: Jessica Kramer

Publishing and Editorial for Technology Dummies

Richard Swadley, Vice President and Executive Group Publisher

Andy Cummings, Vice President and Publisher

Mary Bednarek, Executive Acquisitions Director

Mary C. Corder, Editorial Director

Publishing for Consumer Dummies

Diane Graves Steele, Vice President and Publisher

Joyce Pepple, Acquisitions Director

Composition Services

Gerry Fahey, Vice President of Production Services

Debbie Stailey, Director of Composition Services

Introduction

● ●

*W*elcome to *Instant Messaging For Dummies,* Pocket
Edition. Although lots of books about online
communications are available, most assume that you
have a degree in computer science, would love to know
about every strange and useless wart of the online
world, and enjoy memorizing unpronounceable commands and options. This book is different.

Instead, this book describes what you need to know to
get a handle on staying in touch with your friends,
family, and even new acquaintances online. We tell you
about the resources available for sending instant messages, chatting with friends you find online, and
addressing online communities to discuss common
interests or simply socialize. Also, you get a glimpse of
how text messaging to mobile devices lets you reach
beyond the confines of your computer.

Enjoy . . . and get your fingers ready to make messages!

About This Book

You may not choose to sit down and read this entire
book (although it should be a fine book for the bath-
room), but if you do, we think you'll get a nice
overview of quick messaging options. And when you
run into a question about sending instant messages,
chatting online, communicating with groups and message boards, and so on, check out the Contents at a
Glance to begin looking for your answer.

Pertinent sections include

- ✔ Taking AIM
- ✔ Or Use Yahoo Messenger
- ✔ Embracing Chat Culture
- ✔ Adding Voices and Faces
- ✔ Keeping in Touch, the SMS/MMS Way
- ✔ Texting with an iPhone

Conventions Used in This Book

We try hard not to introduce a technical term without defining it, so when you see a term in *italics*, you've found where we're defining it for you. And because communicating online involves its own language of abbreviations and symbols, we include an appendix that lists the most common ones for you.

When you have to follow a complicated procedure, we spell it out step by step wherever possible. We then tell you what happens in response and what your options are. If you have to type something, it appears in the book in **boldface**. Type it just as it appears and then press the Enter key.

When you have to choose commands from menus, we write File➪Exit when we want you to choose the File command from the menu bar and then choose the Exit command from the menu that appears.

When we talk about a Web site, the *URL* (Uniform Resource Locator), or online address, appears in `monofont`, for example, `www.yahoo.com`.

Who Are You?

In writing this book, we made a few assumptions about you:

- ✔ You have or would like to have access to the Internet.
- ✔ You want to stay in touch with friends, family, and so on by instant messaging.
- ✔ You aren't interested in becoming the world's next great online expert, at least not this week.

Icons Used in This Book

 Indicates that a nifty little shortcut or time-saver is explained.

 Indicates something to file away in your memory archive.

 Gaack! We found out about this the hard way! Don't let it happen to you!

Where to Go from Here

That's all you need to know to get started. Whenever you hit a snag with instant messaging, just look up the topic in the Contents at a Glance. You'll either have the problem solved in a flash or know where you need to go to find some expert help.

4

Part I

Chatting via Text

● ●

In This Part

▶ Typing to one friend at a time

▶ Checking out instant messaging options

▶ Branching out with chat rooms and mailing lists

● ●

*I*nstant messaging (IM'ing) lets you type short messages that appear in a window on someone else's computer. It's faster than e-mail but slightly less intrusive than a phone call, so far fewer people have their secretaries screen their IMs.

This part describes how to use the most popular IM system: AOL Instant Messenger (*AIM,* for short), which is one of the simplest chat systems around. This book describes AIM version 6. If you use AOL, you can use either the separate AIM program we describe here or the AIM part of the regular AOL program (which does the same things although the windows are a little different).

Other IM programs — for example, Windows Messenger and Yahoo Messenger — work similarly to AIM and have similar features. Also, you can find some services (such as Trillian) that allow you to chat with any of your friends regardless of the IM programs they use.

Instant-message programs open a new window when one of your buddies sends you a message. If you have a program that blocks pop-up windows in your browser, IM windows aren't affected because pop-up blockers block only Web browser pop-ups.

In addition to traditional instant messaging programs, this part introduces you to some other forms of communication, including mailing lists, message boards, and online chat.

Taking AIM

If you're an AOL user, you're already set up for instant messages. If not, you have to install the AIM program. AOL subscribers can also run the AIM program and use their AOL screen names when they're logged in to another kind of Internet account.

AOL, hyper-aggressive marketing organization that it is, has arranged for AIM to be bundled with a lot of other packages. If you don't have it, visit www.aim.com and follow the directions on the Web page to download it.

When you install AIM, you have to choose a screen name — which can be up to 16 letters long (be creative so that yours doesn't collide with one of the 40 million names already in use) — and a password. You also have to enter your e-mail address. AOL, refreshingly, doesn't want any more personal information. The e-mail address you give has to be real; AOL sends a confirmation message to that address, and you must reply or else your screen name is deleted.

Normally, AIM runs in the background whenever you're online. If it isn't running, click the AIM icon on your desktop.

The first time you use AIM, you enter your AIM or AOL screen name, as shown in the left part of Figure 1-1. Type your screen name and password and click Sign In.

 If you want to use AIM every time you're online, select the Save Password and Auto Sign In check boxes before signing on, and AIM signs you on automatically in the future. After you sign in, you see the AIM window, shown on the right of Figure 1-1.

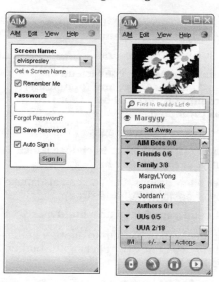

Figure 1-1: Signing on to AIM and the AIM window.

Getting your buddies organized

First you create your Buddy List, and then you can send messages. When AIM opens, you see your *Buddy List* — that is, other AIM users you like to chat with. The window shows which of your many buddies are online now (everyone who's not currently listed in the Offline category).

What? None of your pals appears? You need to add your friends' AOL or AIM screen names to your Buddy List, as follows:

1. **In the AIM window, press Ctrl+D or choose Edit⇨Add Buddy from the menu.**

   The New Buddy window appears.

2. **Type a nickname to use for your friend or coworker, an AIM username, and (optionally) a cell phone number (preceded by +1 for U.S. numbers), as prompted.**

   AIM can send IMs as text messages to cell phones.

3. **Click the Buddy Group button to choose which group to put your new buddy in.**

   AOL provides a few groups, but you can also make your own, by choosing Edit⇨Add Group.

4. **Click Save to add your friend as a buddy.**

You can drag a buddy from one group to another in the Buddy List or get rid of a buddy (by clicking the buddy and then pressing Delete).

Getting buddy-buddy online

To send a message to someone, double-click the buddy's name to open a message window, type the message, and click the Send button or press Enter. AIM pops up a window (shown on Figure 1-2) on the recipient's machine and plays a little song, and you and your buddy can type back and forth. When you're done, close the message window.

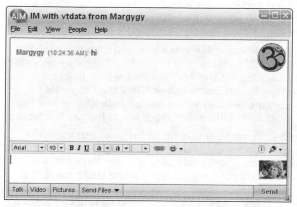

Figure 1-2: Chatting using AIM.

Making noise with AIM

After you establish a conversation using AIM, you can switch to voice (assuming that both parties have computers equipped with microphones and speakers). Click the Talk button and click Connect. Your friend sees a window asking whether he wants to make a direct connection with you.

If your friend accepts the invitation, you can chat using the microphone and speakers on your PC. Click Disconnect when you're done talking. See the section

"Adding Voices and Faces," in Part II, for more about both voice and video on AIM.

Buzz off

AOL evidently has a lot of ill-mannered users, because AIM has a system for warning and blocking users you don't like. If someone sends you an annoying message, you can choose People⟳Ignore in the chat window.

What if someone IMs you when you aren't online? You can tell AIM to show you missed messages by choosing Edit⟳Settings in the AIM window, which displays the Setting – Buddy List window. Click the Offline IM tab, choose the settings you want, and click Save. AIM can save up to 40 offline messages for as long as two weeks.

Sending someone an instant message is the online equivalent of walking up to someone on the street and starting a conversation. If it's someone you know, it's one thing; if not, it's usually an intrusion. Unless you have a compelling reason, don't send instant messages to people you don't know who haven't invited you to do so. Don't say anything that you wouldn't say in an analogous situation on the street.

You can fine-tune who you let send messages to you: Choose Edit⟳Settings, and then click the Privacy tab. You can specify the IM messages you receive in various ways:

- ✔ Limit them to messages from people on your Buddy List.

- ✔ Permit IM access to specific people.

- ✔ Block IM access from specific people. You can also add or delete people from your Block list.

We recommend choosing Allow Only Users on My Buddy List unless you like being contacted by total strangers at inconvenient moments.

The more the merrier — chatting with a group

AIM doesn't limit you to chatting with one person at a time. You can have several chat windows open at the same time, and have separate chats in each window. It can make you crazy, though, keeping track of a bunch of conversations, but teenagers do it every day.

An alternative is to have one chat window for more than just one other person. In a chat window, you can choose People➪Start a Buddy Chat and type the screen names of people you want to invite into a group chat window. AIM opens a new tab in your chat window and sends invitations to your buddies, and, assuming that they click Accept, you're all in!

You can control whether your multiple chats appear in separate windows or as separate tabs in one window. Choose View➪Ungroup All Tabs to make separate windows, or View➪Regroup All Tabs to display all chats in one window.

AIM on your phone

You can tell AIM to forward messages to your cell phone via text message. Choose Edit➪Settings, and then click the Mobile tab. Click Register a Mobile Device to display the signup page in your Web browser. AIM sends a text message to your phone with a code that you must type on the registration page, to prove that the phone is really yours.

If you pay to receive text messages or you don't want to get them from all your AIM buddies, choose Edit⇨ Settings again, click the Mobile tab again, and choose whether to receive text messages from everyone on your Buddy List, only people on a Mobile Buddy List that you can set up, or everyone in the known universe (not recommended for your sanity).

Or Use Windows (Live) Messenger

Someone at Microsoft noticed that instant messaging was a niche in which the company didn't have the dominant program, and so they decided to issue everyone a copy of theirs. Windows XP comes with the latest instant-messaging program, Windows Messenger (which used to be named MSN Messenger), whereas Windows Vista has a Windows Live Messenger Download command on the Start menu.

Windows Live Messenger interconnects with Yahoo Messenger, supports voice and video, and sends text messages to cell phones. It also has a nice Sharing Folder feature that allows you and a friend to share photos and other files.

Versions are available for Windows and Macs. Unless all your friends use Windows or Yahoo Messenger, there's little reason to use it — but if they do (and you want to), you can download it from `http://get. live.com/messenger`.

 We recommend that you decline all the other programs that come along with Windows Live Messenger, by deselecting their check boxes during installation.

After Windows Live Messenger is installed, you can run it by choosing Start⇨Windows Live Messenger. You sign in with your free Windows Live ID (previously known as a .NET Passport), if you created one; this account is the same one you use to read Hotmail, a type of Web mail account.

The Windows Live Messenger program, shown on the left side of Figure 1-3, works similarly to AIM, with a buddy (contact) list and chat windows. With this program, you

- ✔ Add people to your contact list by specifying their Windows Live e-mail addresses (at Live.com or Hotmail.com) or their Yahoo e-mail addresses at Yahoo.com.

- ✔ Right-click a contact name and choose how to contact them — IM, e-mail, voice call, or video call (if you have a webcam).

You can make phone calls from your computer, but the calls aren't free.

Or Use Yahoo Messenger

Yahoo, the popular Web site, has its own instant-message program, named Yahoo Messenger. It pioneered multiperson voice and video chats back in 2001. We've held six-person voice-and-video conference calls using Yahoo Messenger for a total cost of $0.

Yahoo Messenger, which also has a photo-sharing feature, can communicate with Windows Live Messenger, so there's no reason to install both programs. Yahoo Messenger can make and receive voice calls to real telephones, although it costs money. You can also use Yahoo Messenger to join Yahoo chat rooms.

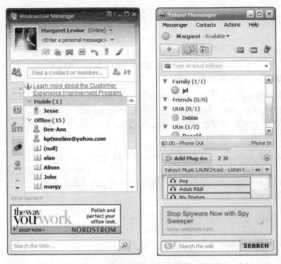

Figure 1-3: Windows Live Messenger and Yahoo Messenger look a lot like AIM.

To get the program, go to http://messenger. yahoo.com and follow the directions to download and install it. Yahoo Messenger is available in many versions, including versions for Windows, Macs, UNIX, and Palm, and a version that runs as a Flash applet in your Web browser — on *any* system that has a Flash-enabled browser.

When you download the program, it installs automatically. To log in, you create a free Yahoo ID for yourself. Go to the http://messenger.yahoo.com Web site and click the Sign In link if you already have a Yahoo ID, or click the Sign Up link if you don't. You can use your Yahoo ID for free Web mail, too.

 We recommend clicking Custom Install during the installation and choosing to install only Yahoo Messenger, without the other miscellaneous programs. (Why glop up your computer?)

Yahoo Messenger, shown on the right side of Figure 1-3, looks and acts very much like AIM:

- Choose Contact⇨Add a Contact to add your friends who use Yahoo or Windows Messenger.

- Right-click a contact and choose how you want to communicate with that person — chat, text message to her cell phone, voice message, or phone call to her telephone number.

- After you're chatting, you can click the Conference button to add other people, or choose Actions⇨View Webcam to view each other's webcams.

 If you don't want to install a chat program, you can use Yahoo Messenger from your browser — go to the http://webmessenger.yahoo.com site to try it out. As of mid-2007, it provided only text chat.

Or Use Them All with Trillian

Unfortunately, the instant-message systems don't always talk to one another. Because the goal of all these systems is to help you stay in touch with your friends, use whichever one they use.

If you aren't sure which messenger your friends use, AOL Instant Messenger is a good bet because it's easy to set up and works automatically with any AOL user; it's the same system that AOL uses internally. AIM, Yahoo Messenger, and Windows Messenger have similar features because when one adds something, the others tend to follow suit.

All three are free; support text, voice, and video; and allow more than two people to chat. (We've held meetings on Yahoo Messenger with six people on voice and two on video and everyone typing snide comments at the same time.) If you have Windows XP or Vista, you already have Windows Messenger, which comes preinstalled.

Use whichever system your friends use. If you're really message-mad or you have friends on more than one system, you can run more than one messaging program at the same time. While we were writing this part, we had Windows Messenger, AOL Instant Messenger, and Yahoo Messenger all running at once. It was an awful lot of blinking and flashing, but it worked.

Better yet, use a program that speaks all three IM languages. We know of and like two such programs; both are free. They are Pidgin, at www.pidgin.im, and Trillian, at www.ceruleanstudios.com, and they simultaneously handle every IM system you've ever heard of.

Trillian tries to install a bunch of extra applications and toolbars when you install it; just say *No* unless you're sure you want them. Pidgin is plain old-fashioned freeware — no ads, no begging. For Mac users, Adium from www.adiumx.com is the Mac version of Pidgin.

When Chatting One on One Just Won't Do

Typing or talking to a few people is fun and interesting, but for really good gossip, you need a group. Fortunately, the Internet offers limitless opportunities to find like-minded people and discuss anything you can imagine.

Clubs, churches, and other groups use the Internet to hold meetings. Hobbyists and fans talk about an amazing variety of topics, from knitting to *American Idol* and everything in between. People with medical problems support each other and exchange tips. You get the idea — anything that people want to talk about is now under intense discussion somewhere on the Net.

You can talk with groups of people on the Internet in lots of ways, including these:

- ✔ **E-mail mailing lists,** in which you exchange messages by e-mail.

- ✔ **Web-based message boards,** where messages appear on Web pages.

- ✔ **Social-networking sites,** like MySpace and Facebook.

- ✔ **Usenet newsgroups** (the original Internet discussion groups), which you read with a *newsreading program.* To find a group, go to http://groups.google.com on the Web and search for topics that interest you.

This section tells you how to participate in Internet-based discussions using e-mail mailing lists and Web message boards.

Mailing lists: Are you sure that this isn't junk mail?

An e-mail mailing list is quite different from a snail-mail mailing list. Yes, both distribute messages to the people on the list, but the messages on most e-mail mailing lists contain discussions among the subscribers rather than junk mail and catalogs.

Here's how an e-mail mailing list works. The list has its own, special e-mail address, and anything someone sends to that address is sent to all the people on the list. Because these people in turn often respond to the messages, the result is a running conversation.

For example, if the authors of this book hosted a discussion called *chocolate-lovers,* about the use and abuse of chocolate, and if the list-server program ran at lists.gurus.com, the list address would be chocolate-lovers@lists.gurus.com. (We do run a bunch of lists, but not one about chocolate. Yet.)

Mailing lists fall into three categories:

- **Discussion:** Every subscriber can post a message, which leads to freewheeling discussions and can include a certain number of off-topic messages.

- **Moderated:** A moderator reviews each message before it is distributed. The moderator can stop unrelated, redundant, or clueless postings from wasting everyone's time.

> ✔ **Announcement-only:** Only the moderator posts messages. Announcement mailing lists are essentially online newsletters.

Someone is in charge of every mailing list: the *list manager*. The list manager is in charge of helping people on and off the list, answering questions about the list, and hosting the discussion. If you have a problem with a list, write a *nice* message to the list manager. The list manager's address is usually the same as the list address with the addition of *owner-* at the beginning or *-request* just before the @. For example, the manager of the `chocoloate-lovers@lists.gurus.com` list would be `chocoloate-lovers-request@lists.gurus.com`.

Most list managers are volunteers who sometimes eat, sleep, and work regular jobs as well as maintain mailing lists. If getting a response takes longer than you want, be patient. *Don't* send cranky follow-ups — they just cheese off the list manager.

Mailing list tricks

With most lists, you can subscribe, unsubscribe, and change your subscription settings from the Web — you go to a Web page and fill out a form.

Don't delete the chatty, informative mailing-list welcome message that tells you about all the commands you can use when you're dealing with the list. For one thing, it tells you how to get *off* the mailing list if it isn't to your liking.

Some of the fine points of dealing with mailing lists include

- ✔ **Responding to messages:** Often, you receive an interesting message from a list and want to respond to it. Fortunately, you're in charge of whether your reply goes to just the subscriber who posted the message or to the entire subscriber list. When you start to create a reply, your mail program should show you the address to which it's replying. Check the To and Cc fields to make sure that you're sending your message where you want.

- ✔ **Waiting before sending a message:** After you subscribe to a list, don't send anything to it until you read it for a week. By waiting, you can determine which topics people really discuss and the tone of the list. Trust us — the list has been getting along without your insights since it began, and it can get along without them for one more week.

- ✔ **Dealing with one person without involving the entire group:** If you don't like what another person is posting (for example, some newbie is posting blank messages or "unsubscribe me" messages or is ranting interminably about a topic), e-mail the person *privately* and ask him to stop, or e-mail the list manager and ask that person to intervene.

Posting to message boards

Mailing lists are great if you want to receive messages by e-mail, but some people prefer to read messages on the Web. These folks are in luck: *Message boards* are Web-based discussion groups that post messages on Web sites. They're also called *discussion boards*, *forums*, or *communities*.

Like mailing lists, some message boards are readable only by subscribers, some allow only subscribers to post, and some are *moderated* (that is, a moderator must approve messages before they appear on the message board). Other message boards are more like bulletin boards: Anyone can post at any time, and there's no continuity to the messages or feeling of community among the people who post.

Here are some of our favorite Web-based discussion sites:

✔ **About.com, at** www.about.com: About.com hires semipro experts in a wide variety of fields to host sites about each field. For example, the knitting site at http://knitting.about.com is run by a world-class knitter who posts articles and patterns and hosts one or more message boards about knitting. (See Figure 1-4.)

✔ **Google Groups, at** http://groups.google.com: Google Groups started as a way for people to participate in Usenet newsgroups via the Web, but Google provides a way to set up new groups, too.

✔ **MSN Groups, at** http://groups.msn.com: MSN Groups includes message boards, live chat rooms, and other information. To join a group, you need to sign up for a free .NET Passport.

✔ **Yahoo Groups, at** http://groups.yahoo.com: Yahoo Groups include message boards and file libraries, and you can read the messages either on the Web site or by e-mail. To join, you must first sign up for a free Yahoo ID, which also gets you a mailbox and free Web space — what a deal!

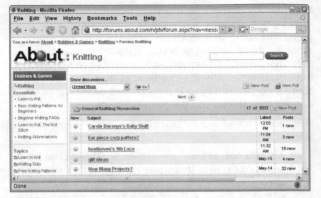

Figure 1-4: The About.com knitting message board.

Most good message boards require you to register before you can subscribe, which means that you choose a username and password, possibly provide your e-mail address, and respond to a message sent to that address. To subscribe to a community on one of these Web sites, just follow the instructions on the site.

Embracing Chat Culture

Online chat is similar to talking on an old-fashioned party line (or CB radio). Online chat differs from IM chat because it's public and you usually don't know the other people in the discussion.

You begin chatting by entering an area of the Internet called an electronic *chat room* or *channel*. After you join a room, you can read on-screen what people are saying and then add your own comments just by typing them and clicking Send. Several people participate in the chat and may type at the same time, so each contribution is presented on-screen in the order received.

Look who's chatting

Chatting is pretty much the same from system to system, although the participants vary. Each chat room has a name; with luck, the name is an indication of what the chatters there are talking about or what they have in common. Some channels have names such as *lobby,* and the people there are probably just being sociable.

Which groups of people you can chat with depends on which chat systems you connect to. Here are a few places you can find groups of people chatting online:

- ✔ **America Online:** If you have an America Online account, you can chat with other AOL users.

- ✔ **Skype and other VoIP systems:** If you use Skype (described in Part II), you can choose the Live tab to join a public voice chat, or choose Chats⇨Start Public Chat to start your own.

- ✔ **Web sites:** Some Web sites include chat rooms, using a plug-in program that allows people to type at each other.

- ✔ **Yahoo Messenger:** In Yahoo Messenger, you can choose Messenger⇨Yahoo Chat.

If one of the people in a chat room seems like someone you want to know better, you can ask to establish a *private room* or *direct connection,* which is a private conversation between you and the other person and not much different from instant messaging.

As in society at large, online chat involves some contact with strangers. Most encounters are with more-or-less reasonable folks. For the rest, common sense dictates that you keep your wits about you — and your private information private.

Online chat etiquette

Chatting etiquette isn't that much different from e-mail etiquette, and common sense is your best guide. Here are some additional chatting tips:

✔ **Don't hurt anyone.** A real person with real feelings is at the other end of the computer-chat connection. Don't insult people, don't use foul language, and don't respond to people who do.

✔ **Be cautious.** You really have no idea who the other people are. Remember, too, that people might be hanging out in chat rooms quietly collecting information, and you might not notice them because they never say anything.

✔ **Keep your messages short and to the point.** Also, if you want to talk to someone in private, send a message saying hi, identifying yourself, and stating what you want to talk about.

✔ **Create a profile with selected information about yourself.** Most chat systems have provisions for creating profiles (personal information) that other members can access. You don't have to tell everything about yourself, but what you do say should be truthful. The one exception is role-playing chat, where everyone is acting out a fantasy character.

Don't give out your last name, phone number, or address. Extra caution is necessary for kids: A kid should never enter her age, hometown, school, last name, phone number, or address.

✔ **Move on.** If the tone of conversation in one chat room offends or bores you, try another. As in real life, you run into lots of people in chat rooms that you *don't* want to meet — and you don't have to stay there.

Getting Your Chat On

Your first time in a chat room can seem stupid or daunting or both. Here are some things you can do to get through your first encounters:

✔ Remember that when you enter a chat room, a conversation is probably already in progress. You don't know what went on before you arrived.

✔ Wait a minute or two to see a page full of exchanges so that you can understand some of the context before you start writing.

✔ Read messages for a while to figure out what's happening before sending a message to a chat group. Reading without saying anything is known as *lurking.* When you finally venture to say something, you're *de-lurking.* Lurking isn't necessarily a bad thing, but be aware that you might not always have the privacy you think you have.

✔ Some chat systems enable you to indicate people to ignore. Messages from these chatters no longer appear on your screen, although other members' replies to them do appear. This is usually the best way to deal with obnoxious chatters.

✔ Scroll up to see older messages if you have to, but remember that on most systems, after you have scrolled up, no new messages appear until you scroll back down.

The original chat rooms consisted entirely of people typing messages to each other. Newer chat systems include *voice chat* (which requires you to have a microphone and speakers on your computer) and even video (which requires a webcam if you want other people to be able to see you).

Whatever chat service you use, the idea is the same — you read other people's messages and chime in with your own. Web-based chat sites have Java-based chat programs that your browser can download and run automatically. Some other Web chat sites require that you download a plug-in or ActiveX control to add chat capability to your browser.

Some Web chat sites include

✔ ICG Chat at www.icq.com/icqchat

✔ MSN Groups at http://groups.msn.com

✔ Userplane at www.userplane.com, which supports text, voice, and video chat

Many other Web sites have chats on the specific topic of the site. Search for **chat** at http://.dmoz.org or www.google.com for a variety of chat venues.

Most chat sites have directories or search boxes so that you can find a group talking about a topic of interest. And most Web-based chat pages have a large window that displays the ongoing conversation, a smaller window that displays the screen names of the participants, and a text area where you type your messages. Figure 1-5 shows a chat room at Userplane.com.

After you type your message, press Enter or click Send, and the message appears in the message window for you and everyone else in the chat room.

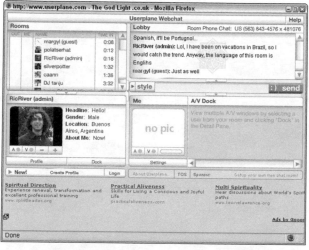

Figure 1-5: The Userplane site hosts lots of chat rooms.

Part II

Adding Sights and Sounds

. . . .

In This Part

▶ Speaking as well as typing

▶ Putting your webcam to work

▶ Skyping and voice chat

. . . .

The big three instant messaging programs — AOL Instant Messenger, Windows (Live) Messenger, and Yahoo Messenger — covered in Part I support voice and video, as well as text-based communication. And Internet phone services (such as Skype) include IM chat capabilities, too.

In this part, we talk about the programs and equipment you need to add audio and video to your instant communications.

Adding Voices and Faces

If you don't want to talk with or see people while you chat — that is, if you don't mind being limited to typing back and forth with your friends — skip this section. If you do want the audiovisual goodies, read on. You can use a webcam with AIM, Yahoo Messenger, and Windows Live Messenger.

Say what? Hooking up the sound

Almost every computer comes with speakers, which are connected to a *sound board* inside the computer. These speakers are what make the various noises that your programs make (like the AOL "You've got mail!" announcement). Most laptops have a built-in microphone, and most desktop computers also have a jack for a microphone. (Check your computer manual or ask almost any teenager for help with this.)

If you don't have a microphone, you can get one that works with almost any computer. A mike should cost less than $20 at your local computer or office supply store.

To test your mike and speakers on a Windows machine, run the Sound Recorder program; try recording yourself and playing it back.

1. **Choose Start⇨All Programs⇨Accessories⇨ Entertainment⇨Sound Recorder.**

2. **Click the red Record button to start recording, and the square Stop button to stop.**

   Talk, sing, or make other noises between your Start and Stop clicks.

3. **Click the triangular Play button to hear what you just recorded.**

   Click Record again to add to the end of your recording. Choose File⇨New to start over and throw away what you recorded.

4. **Choose File⇨Save to save it as a WAV (audio) file.**

We like to make WAV (pronounced *wave*) recordings of our kids saying silly things and e-mail
them — the recordings, not the kids — to their
grandparents.

You can adjust the volume of your microphone (for the
sound coming into the computer) and your speakers or
headphones (for the sound coming out) by choosing
Start⇨All Programs⇨Accessories⇨Entertainment⇨
Volume Control. If a volume control for your microphone doesn't appear, choose Options⇨Properties,
select the Microphone check box so that a check mark
appears, and click OK.

If you want to test how voices from the Net
sound on your computer, type the URL
`http://net.gurus.com/ngc.wav` into your
browser and see what happens. You may need
to click an Open or Open with Default
Application button after the file downloads.

If you can record yourself and hear the recording when
you play it back, you're ready for Internet-based phone
calls or chats!

I see you!

If you want other people to be able to see you during
online conversations, consider getting a *webcam*. This
small digital video camera can connect to a computer.
Webcams come in many sizes and shapes, and prices
run from $30 to $300. More expensive webcams send
higher-quality images at higher speeds and come with
better software. On the other hand, we've had great
luck with a $36 webcam for chatting with friends and
participating in videoconferences.

Most webcams connect to your computer's USB port, a little rectangular plug on the back of the computer. Older computers don't have USB ports. The better cameras connect to special video-capture cards, which you have to open your computer to install. For news and reviews about webcams, see the WebCam.com site at www.webcam.com.

 If you own a digital video camera for taking video of your family and friends, you may be able to connect it to your computer for use as a webcam. Check the manual that came with the camera.

Viewing your chat buddies

When chatting in AIM with one other person, if both you and your friend have webcams set up, you can switch them on for use in your chat. Make sure that AIM knows about your webcam; choose Edit⇨Settings, click the Enhanced IM tab, and see whether the camera appears in the Video setting. (It may just say Default Device.)

To switch on your webcam, click the Video button at the bottom of the chat window. You see a message while AIM sets up the connection, and then your buddy's image appears! You can choose Actions in the video window to control the size of the video image.

Getting a webcam working with Yahoo Messenger, Windows Live Messenger, or Skype (described in the next section) works pretty much the same way as with AIM.

Internet Phones and Voice Chat

For about a decade, Internet phones were just around the corner. If you have a broadband Net connection, you're now near that corner. No Internet phenomenon would be complete without an arcane abbreviation, so this one is *VoIP* (for Voice over Internet Protocol), pronounced either *V-O-I-P* or to sound like a dripping faucet *(voyp)*.

Some kinds of VoIP use a microphone and headphones plugged into the computer, but most people prefer the variety that uses regular phones plugged into a *terminal adapter,* or TA. (The upcoming section, "The hype about Skype" talks about the main exception.)

Signing up

Setting up VoIP phone service is moderately complicated, not unlike setting up regular phone service. You visit a VoIP provider's Web site and go through the signup and setup process, which includes

✔ **Giving your payment info and picking your phone number.** You can choose a phone number where you live or anywhere you want people to be able to call you as a local call.

Most VoIP companies can also *port* your existing phone number away from your old phone company so that you don't have to change your number. (If you later hate your VoIP company, you can port it back, or to a different VoIP company.)

✔ **Connecting your terminal adapter (TA) device.**
After you pay and pick a phone number, the company ships you the TA, which you plug into your
Internet connection. Then you plug a regular
phone into the TA, and you're ready to go.

Several VoIP companies sell combined routers and
VoIP terminal adapters through electronics stores.
In that case, you set up your Internet connection
with the router. Then you use your computer's
Web browser to go to the VoIP company's Web
site to activate the terminal-adapter part of the
router, plug a phone into the phone jack on the
router, and you're ready to go.

VoIP companies vary a lot, with local calling areas rang-
ing from a single U.S. state to all of North America,
Europe, and large parts of Asia. Calls to other cus-
tomers of the same VoIP company are always free, so
you might want to get the same one your friends have.
See our Web site at net.gurus.com/phone for some
suggestions about VoIP companies.

If you have a cable modem, your cable company may
also offer VoIP. If it does, the quality of service is better
than what you get with independent VoIP providers. So,
VoIP through your cable company is worth a close look.

Using your VoIP phone

It's a phone. When it rings, answer it. If you want to call
someone, pick up the phone and dial. Most VoIP companies offer a full suite of phone features, like voice
mail, call forwarding, and caller ID, usually controlled
via a Web page rather than through the phone itself.

The hype about Skype

Skype is a freeware VoIP service owned by eBay. The service is located in Luxembourg, a tiny country in Europe whose main attraction is that it's not anywhere else. You download and install Skype on your computer from www.skype.com, set up a free account, and start using it to talk to other Skype users.

To use Skype, you need a headset with headphones and a microphone, or a handset (which is like a phone handset) plugged into your computer. Skype's voice quality over most broadband is very good, much better than that of a normal phone.

Skype isn't limited to talking to other Skype users. You can also do the following:

✔ **Set up a SkypeOut account** to which you add money — from a credit card or as a bonus included with some computer headsets — and you can then call any normal phone in the world and pay by the minute. Rates are quite low, about 2 cents per minute for the U.S., Canada, or Europe, and don't depend on where you're using Skype, only on where you're calling.

John once called home using his laptop via a WiFi connection in a hotel lobby in Argentina for 2 cents per minute rather than the dollar per minute it would have cost from a payphone.

✔ **Use SkypeIn** — a real phone number for your Skype phone so that people can call you — for a monthly fee.

- ✔ **Hold conference calls** of up to five people, with any combination of Skype users and SkypeOut calls to regular phones. Conference calling includes an IM feature for typing with your friends while talking to them (or even when you're not talking to them).

- ✔ **Set up the chat feature SkypeMe,** in which you fill out a profile, set your online status to SkypeMe, and invite people to call.

Skype users live all over the world, so with luck, you may make some new faraway friends.

Part III

Messaging on the Run

• •

In This Part

▶ Text messaging with a BlackBerry

▶ Doing the same on your iPhone

• •

*O*nline communications (such as instant messaging, Internet phones, and chat) involve wonderful technologies, but you might find yourself in a situation where you don't have access to your computer. So, short of a traditional phone call, what are your alternatives for reaching your friends in an instant?

Read this part and find out about the capabilities of two popular mobile devices: the BlackBerry and the iPhone. Get the inside scoop on using these devices to send and receive text messages while you're on the go.

Keeping in Touch, the SMS/MMS Way

Short Messaging Service (also known as *SMS*, or simply *text messaging*) is so popular these days that you see it used in many TV shows, including the Fox Network's *American Idol,* which lets you vote for the show's contestants by using SMS. Moreover, SMS is an established technology (not a new and unproven thing, in other words) that has been popular for years in Europe and Asia, where the *Global System for Mobile Communication* (GSM) is the technology of choice among cell phone network providers.

In this short messaging service, how short is short? For many phones, the maximum size per message is about 160 characters. If you send more than that, your text is cut off or broken into multiple messages.

Multimedia Messaging Service (MMS) is the latest evolution of SMS. Rather than a simple text message, you can also send someone an audio or video clip.

You need to be aware of the trends and options for text messaging. There is a growing SMS subculture among teenagers and those who jumped onto the bandwagon early. These in-the-know folks use abbreviations that might be difficult for you to understand in the beginning, so don't dive in without your oxygen tank.

Embracing Messaging Shorthand

From the get-go, text messaging sprang up from the wild and crazy world of cell phone users. And those of you who've used a phone lately probably know that phone design revolves around entering phone numbers rather than entering the text to *War and Peace*.

Time for a reality check: On a regular cell phone, three letters share a single key. As you can imagine, trying to bang out even a single paragraph can be a real pain.

Human ingenuity prevails. People have found ways to circumvent the fact that cell phones have such a limited number of keys at their disposal. One strategy that we highlight here involves using abbreviations that allow you to cut down on the amount of text you need to enter. These shorthand words are quickly becoming quite hip, especially among the 14–18-year-old set.

Veteran text messagers (the hip ones, at least) can easily spot someone who is new to SMS technology by how they don't use the right lingo — or use such lingo incorrectly.

A quick preparation goes a long way toward avoiding being labeled *uncool* when it comes to your SMS syntax. Check out the Appendix for the scoop on the basics of SMS-speak.

Texting with Your BlackBerry

Whether you call it SMS, Short Messaging Service, or just plain text messaging, your BlackBerry makes it simple. But before we go over the details, we want to point out to all you BlackBerry Pearl owners that text messaging does pose a challenge for beginners. It's not that it's a difficult task; it's just that it's cumbersome to type the letters by using the limited keypad.

Check out the appendix for abbreviations and symbols you can use to communicate in text messages, as well as in instant messages and online chat.

Sending a text message

After you have the shorthand stuff as well as the smileys under your belt, get your fingers pumped up and ready for action: It's message sending time! Whether it's SMS or a richer audio/video (MMS) message, here's how it's done:

1. **From the BlackBerry Home screen, select Address Book.**

   Address Book opens.

2. **Highlight a contact who has a cell phone number, press the menu key, and select SMS (or MMS) <*Contact Name*> from the menu that appears.**

   The menu item for SMS or MMS is intelligent enough to display the name of the contact. For example, if you choose John Doe, the menu item reads SMS John Doe or MMS John Doe, as shown to the left in Figure 3-1. (Note the space for entering your text message, right underneath the screen heading.)

3. **If you chose MMS, Browse from your multimedia folders and select the audio or video file you want to send.**

   When choosing MMS, this extra step allows you to choose the multimedia file. This is the only difference between SMS and MMS with regards to sending a message.

4. **Type your message.**

   Remember that shorthand business? You should start taking advantage of it the first chance you get. (Practice makes perfect.)

5. **Press the trackball and then select Send from the menu that appears.**

   Your message is sent on its merry way.

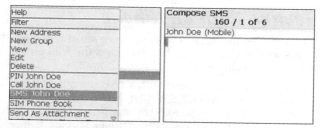

Help		Compose SMS
Filter		160 / 1 of 6
New Address		John Doe (Mobile)
New Group		
View		
Edit		
Delete		
PIN John Doe		
Call John Doe		
SMS John Doe		
SIM Phone Book		
Send As Attachment		

Figure 3-1: Start your text message here.

Viewing a message you receive

If you have an incoming SMS or MMS message, you get
notification just like you do when you receive an e-mail.
Also, like e-mail, the e-mail icon on the top of the Home
screen indicates a new message. In fact, everything
about viewing SMS and MMS messages is pretty much
the same as what you do when reading an e-mail. The
basic run-through is as follows:

1. **Open Messages.**

2. **Scroll to the unread message.**

3. **Press the trackball.**

4. **Bob's your uncle: The message appears on-
   screen.**

You can customize how your BlackBerry noti-
fies you when you receive an SMS message.
Look for the SMS notification options while
customizing your profile.

Texting with an iPhone

The Text application lets you exchange short text messages with any cell phone that supports the SMS protocol (which is almost all cell phones today).

Typing text on a cell phone with a 12-key numeric keypad is an unnatural act, which is why many people have never sent a single SMS text message. The iPhone will change that. The intelligent virtual keyboard makes it easy to compose short text messages, and the big, bright, high-resolution screen makes it a pleasure to read them.

But before we get to the part where you send or receive SMS messages, let's go over some SMS basics:

✔ Both sender and receiver need SMS-enabled mobile phones. Your iPhone qualifies, as does almost any mobile phone made in the past four or five years. Keep in mind that if you send SMS messages to folks with phones that don't support SMS, they'll never get your message — nor will they know you even sent a message.

✔ Some phones (not the iPhone, of course) limit SMS messages to 160 characters. If you try to send a longer message to one of these phones, your message may be truncated or split into multiple shorter messages. The point is that it's a good idea to keep SMS messages brief.

✔ Most iPhone plans include 200 SMS text messages per month. If you use more than 200, you'll be charged extra for each message over 200.

Each individual message in a conversation counts against this total, even if it's only a one-word reply such as "OK," or "CUL8R" (which is teenager for "see you later").

✔ You can increase the number of SMS messages in your plan for a few more dollars a month. This is almost always less expensive than paying for them a la carte.

✔ You can send or receive SMS messages only over the AT&T network. Put another way, SMS messages can't be sent or received over a WiFi connection.

Okay. Now that we have that out of the way, let's start with how to *send* SMS text messages.

You send me: Sending SMS text messages

Tap the Text (SMS) icon on the Home screen to launch the Text application, and then tap the little pencil and paper icon in the top-right corner of the screen to start a new text message.

At this point, the To field is active and awaiting your input. You can do three things at this point:

✔ If the recipient isn't in your Contacts list, type his or her cell phone number.

✔ If the recipient is in your Contacts list, type the first few letters of the name. A list of matching contacts appears. Scroll through it if necessary and tap the name of the contact.

The more letters you type, the shorter the list becomes.

✔ Tap the blue plus icon on the right side of the To field to select a name from your contact list.

There's a fourth option if you want to compose the message first and address it later. Tap the text entry field, which is just above the keyboard and to the left of the Send button, and type your message. When you've finished typing, you'll need to tap the To field and use one of the preceding techniques to address your message.

When you finish addressing and composing, tap the Send button to send your message on its merry way. And that's all there is to it.

Being a golden receiver: Receiving SMS text messages

First things first. If you want to hear an alert sound when you receive an SMS text message, tap the Settings icon on your Home screen, tap Sounds, and then turn on the New Text Message item. (If you don't want to hear an alert when an SMS message arrives, turn it off.) Remember, though, that even if the New Text Message option is turned on, you won't hear an alert sound when an SMS message arrives if the Ring/Silent switch is off.

Two things happen when you receive an SMS text message:

✔ **When you wake up your iPhone,** all or part of the text will appear on the unlock screen.

✔ **After you unlock the phone,** the Text icon on the Home screen displays the number of unread messages.

To read and respond to your message, follow these steps:

1. **Tap the Text icon.**

   The Text Messages screen appears.

2. **Tap the message to read it.**

3. **If you want to reply to the message, tap the text entry field to the left of the Send button.**

   The keyboard appears.

4. **Type a reply and then tap Send.**

Your conversation is saved as a series of text bubbles. Your messages appear on the right side of the screen in green bubbles; the other person's messages appear on the left in gray bubbles, as shown in Figure 3-2.

You can delete a conversation in two ways:

✓ **If you're viewing the conversation:** Tap the Clear button at the top right of the conversation screen.

✓ **If you're viewing the list of text messages:** Tap the Edit button at the top left of the Text Messages list, and then tap the red minus icon that appears next to the conversation.

Smart SMS tricks

Here are some more things you can do with SMS text messages:

✓ To send an SMS text message to someone in your Favorites or Recents list, tap the Phone icon on the Home screen, and then tap Favorites or Recents, respectively. Tap the blue > icon to the right of a name or number, and then tap Text Message at the bottom of the Info screen.

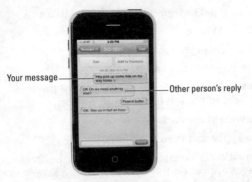

Your message —

— Other person's reply

Figure 3-2: This is what an SMS conversation looks like.

✔ To call or e-mail someone to whom you've sent an SMS text message, tap the Text icon on the Home screen, and then tap the message in the Text Messages list. Tap the Call button at the top of the conversation to call the person, or tap the Contact Info button and then tap an e-mail address to send an e-mail.

   You can use this technique only if the contact has an e-mail address.

✔ To add someone to whom you've sent an SMS text message to your Contacts list, tap his name or phone number in the Text Messages list and then tap the Add to Contacts button.

✔ If an SMS message includes a URL, tap it to open that Web page in Safari.

✔ If an SMS message includes a phone number, tap it to call that number.

- ✔ If an SMS message includes an e-mail address, tap it to open a pre-addressed e-mail message in Mail.

- ✔ If an SMS message includes a street address, tap it to see a map in Maps.

And that's all there is to it. You are now an official SMS text message maven.

Must-Know Abbreviations and Smileys

• •

*T*yping is way slower than talking, so when people IM or participate in online chat, they tend to abbreviate wildly.

Check Out the IM Lingo

Many chat abbreviations are the same as those used in e-mail. Because IM is live, however, some are unique; check out the IM abbreviations in Table 1.

In addition to using the abbreviations in Table 1, chatters sometimes use simple shorthand abbreviations, as in If u cn rd ths ur rdy 2 chat.

Table 1	IM and Chat Shorthand
Abbreviation	*What It Means*
2D4	To die for
2G4U	Too good for you
2L8	Too late
4E	Forever
4YEO	For your eyes only
A3	Anytime, anywhere, anyplace

(continued)

Table 1 *(continued)*

Abbreviation	What It Means
AFAIK	As far as I know
AFK	Away from keyboard
ASAP	As soon as possible
A/S/L	Age/sex/location (response may be 35/f/LA)
ATM	At the moment
ATW	At the weekend
AWHFY	Are we having fun yet?
B4	Before
BAK	Back at keyboard
BBFN	Bye-bye for now
BBL	Be back later
BBS	Be back soon
BCNU	Be seeing you
BFF	Best friend forever
BG	Big grin
BION	Believe it or not
BOL	Best of luck
BOT	Back on topic
BRB	Be right back
BRT	Be right there
BTW	By the way
CMON	Come on

Abbreviation	What It Means
CU	See you
CUL8R	See you later
CUS	See you soon
CYBER	A chat conversation of a prurient nature (short for *cybersex*)
FTF or F2F	Face to face
FC	Fingers crossed
FCFS	First come, first served
FOAF	Friend of a friend
FWIW	For what it's worth
GAL	Get a life
GG	Good game
GR8	Great
GSOH	Good sense of humor
H2CUS	Hope to see you soon
IC	In character (playing a role)
IDK	I don't know
IGGIE	To set the Ignore feature, as in "I've iggied SmartMouthSam"
IM	Instant message
IMHO	In my humble opinion
IMO	In my opinion
IOU	I owe you
IOW	In other words

(continued)

Table 1 *(continued)*

Abbreviation	What It Means
J/K	Just kidding
KISS	Keep it simple, stupid
LOL	Laughing out loud
LTNS	Long time no see
NP	No problem
OIC	Oh, I see
OOC	Out of character (an RL aside during RP)
PM	Private message (same as IM)
RL	Real life (opposite of RP)
ROTFL	Rolling on the floor laughing
RUOK	Are you OK?
RP	Role playing (acting out a character)
TMOZ	Tomorrow
TTFN	Ta-ta for now!
W4U	Waiting for you
W8	Wait
WB	Welcome back
WTF?	What the heck?
WTG	Way to go!

1M with Feeling

Table 2 lists some common *emoticons* — also called *smileys* — which are funky combinations of punctuation used to depict the emotional inflection of the sender.

If at first you don't see what they are, try tilting your head to the left.

Table 2	Smileys and Their Meanings
Smiley	*Meaning*
:)	Happy, smiling
:-)	Happy, smiling, with nose
:D	Laughing
:-D	Laughing, with nose
{{{{bob}}}}	A hug for Bob
:(or :-(	Frown
:'(	Crying
:'-)	Tears due to laughter
:-)8	Smiling with bow tie
;)	Winking
;-)	Winking, with nose
0:-)	I'm an angel (male)
0*-)	I'm an angel (female)
}:>	I'm a devil
8-)	Cool, with sunglasses
:-!	Foot in mouth

(continued)

Table 2 *(continued)*

Smiley	Meaning
>-)	Evil grin
:-x	Kiss on the lips
*** or xox	Kisses
(((H)))	Hugs
@>--;--	Rose
:b	Tongue out
;b	Tongue out with a wink
:-&	Tongue tied
-!-	Sleepy
:-<	Super sad
:-0	Yell, gasp
:-@	Scream, what?
:-(o)	Shouting
|-0	Yawn
:----(	Liar, long nose
%-(	Confused
:-|	Determined
:-()	Talking
:-ozz	Bored
@@	Eyes
%-)	Cross-eyed
|@@|	Face

Smiley	Meaning
#:-)	Hair is a mess
&:-)	Hair is curly
$-)	Yuppie
:-($)	Put your money where your mouth is
<----	Action marker that appears before a phrase indicating what you're doing (<----eating pizza, for example)

With more than 1,300 titles to choose from, we've got a Dummies Book for wherever you are in life!

Business/Career

Becoming a Personal Trainer For Dummies	9780764556845	$19.99/$23.99 CAN
Freelancing For Dummies	9780764553691	$21.99/$29.99 CAN
Getting Your Book Published For Dummies	9780764552571	$19.99/$25.99 CAN
Paralegal Career For Dummies	9780471799566	$24.99/$29.99 CAN
Real Estate License Exams For Dummies	9780764576232	$16.99/$19.99 CAN
Success as a Real Estate Agent For Dummies	9780471799559	$21.99/$25.99 CAN
Writing Children's Books For Dummies	9780764537288	$19.99/$25.99 CAN
Exercise Balls For Dummies	9780764556234	$21.99/$28.99 CAN

Fitness

Fit Over 40 For Dummies	9780764553059	$19.99/$23.99 CAN
Fit Pregnancy For Dummies	9780764558290	$19.99/$28.99 CAN
Fitness Walking For Dummies	9780764551925	$19.99/$28.99 CAN
Stretching For Dummies	9780470067413	$16.99/$19.99 CAN
Weight Training For Dummies, 3rd Edition	9780471768456	$21.99/$25.99 CAN
Workouts For Dummies	9780764551246	$21.99/$25.99 CAN
Yoga with Weights For Dummies	9780471749370	$21.99/$28.99 CAN

Crafts & Hobbies

Candy Making For Dummies	9780764597343	$19.99/$23.99 CAN
Crochet Patterns For Dummies	9780470045558	$19.99/$23.99 CAN
Holiday Entertaining For Dummies	9780764552359	$19.99/$29.99 CAN
Home Decorating For Dummies, 2nd Edition	9780764541568	$19.99/$23.99 CAN
Jewelry Making & Beading For Dummies	9780764525711	$19.99/$25.99 CAN
Knitting Patterns For Dummies	9780470045565	$19.99/$23.99 CAN
Reconstructing Clothes For Dummies	9780470127674	$19.99/$23.99 CAN
Scrapbooking For Dummies	9780764572081	$19.99/$25.99 CAN
Window Treatments & Slipcovers For Dummies	9780764584480	$19.99/$23.99 CAN

Dummies Books — Plain-English Solutions for Everyday Challenges

Home & Business Computer Basics

Title	ISBN	Price
Excel 2007 All-in-One Desk Reference For Dummies	9780470037386	$29.99/$35.99 CAN
MacBook For Dummies	9780470048597	$21.99/$25.99 CAN
Office 2007 All-in-One Desk Reference For Dummies	9780471782797	$29.99/$35.99 CAN
PCs All-in-One Desk Reference For Dummies, 4th Edition	9780470223383	$29.99/$35.99 CAN
PCs For Dummies, 11th Edition	9780470137284	$21.99/$25.99 CAN
Troubleshooting Your PC For Dummies	9780764516696	$24.99/$37.99 CAN
Upgrading & Fixing PCs For Dummies	9780764516658	$21.99/$32.99 CAN
Windows XP All-in-One Desk Reference For Dummies	9780471749417	$29.99/$35.99 CAN
Windows Vista For Dummies	9780471754213	$21.99/$25.99 CAN
Windows Vista For Dummies, Quick Reference	9780471783268	$16.99/$19.99 CAN
Word 2007 For Dummies	9780470036587	$21.99/$25.99 CAN
CD & DVD Recording For Dummies	9780764516276	$21.99/$32.99 CAN

Internet & Digital Media

Title	ISBN	Price
Digital Photography All-in-One Desk Reference For Dummies, 3rd Edition	9780470037430	$35.99/$47.99 CAN
Geneology For Dummies	9780764508073	$24.99/$37.99 CAN
Internet All-in-One Desk Reference For Dummies	9780764516597	$29.99/$44.99 CAN
Internet For Dummies, 11th Edition	9780470121740	$21.99/$25.99 CAN
Search Engine Optimization For Dummies, 2nd Edition	9780471979982	$24.99/$29.99 CAN
iPhone For Dummies	9780470174692	$21.99/$25.99 CAN
AppleTV For Dummies	9780470173626	$21.99/$25.99 CAN
Photoshop Elements 2 For Dummies	9780764516757	$21.99/$32.99 CAN
YouTube For Dummies	9780470149256	$21.99/$25.99 CAN

Graphics & Web Development

Title	ISBN	Price
Flash CS3 For Dummies	9780470121009	$24.99/$29.99 CAN
ASP.NET For Dummies	9780764508660	$24.99/$37.99 CAN
Dreamweaver CS3 For Dummies	9780470114902	$24.99/$29.99 CAN
iMac For Dummies, 4th Edition	9780764584589	$21.99/$25.99 CAN
InDesign CS3 For Dummies	9780470118658	$24.99/$29.99 CAN
Macs For Dummies, 9th Edition	9780470048498	$21.99/$25.99 CAN
Photoshop CS3 All-in-One Desk Reference For Dummies	9780470111956	$39.99/$47.99 CAN
Photoshop CS3 For Dummies	9780470111932	$24.99/$29.99 CAN
PowerPoint 2007 For Dummies	9780470040591	$21.99/$25.99 CAN
Web Design For Dummies, 2nd Edition	9780471781172	$24.99/$31.99 CAN